AF407556

HERE'S HOW TO LIVE FOREVER

"GOOD NIGHT MR. MONKEY, GOOD NIGHT MS. BUNNY...
AND GOOD NIGHT KYLA. SWEET DREAMS. SLEEP WELL, BECAUSE
WE ARE GOING TO GRANDMA AND GRAMPA'S HOUSE IN THE
MORNING," DADDY SAID.

"DADDY, DO YOU HAVE A GRANDMA AND GRAMPA?" ASKED KYLA.

"YES, BUT THEY ARE IN HEAVEN NOW," REPLIED DADDY.

"WHAT DO YOU MEAN, DADDY?" ASKED KYLA.

"WELL, AFTER WE LIVE A
WONDERFUL LIFE, EVENTUALLY
PEOPLE DIE AND GO TO HEAVEN,"
DADDY REPLIED.

KYLA BECAME SCARED,
"DADDY, AM I GOING TO DIE?"

"WELL, UM, YES" REPLIED DADDY,
"BUT NOT UNTIL AFTER YOU'VE
LIVED A NICE LONG...."

"...BUT I WANT TO LIVE FOREVER! I JUST WANT TO LIVE HERE IN OUR HOUSE FOREVER WITH MOMMY, ZOE AND CALLIE, AND PLAY ALL DAY. I WANT TO LIVE FOREVER!!!

DADDY TRIED TO REASSURE KYLA, "DON'T WORRY KYLA, YOU'RE ONLY 5 YEARS OLD. EVERYTHING IS GOING TO BE OK."

"THIS ISN'T WORKING..." DADDY THOUGHT TO HIMSELF.
Waaahh...

"OK KYLA," SAID DADDY,
"I HAVE SOMETHING TO
TELL YOU. I KNOW ALL THE
SECRETS OF HOW TO LIVE
FOREVER.

KYLA LOOKED UP,
"REALLY DADDY? CAN YOU
TEACH ME THE SECRETS?

"KYLA," DADDY ANSWERED,
"I'M GOING TO TEACH YOU ALL
THE SECRETS ON HOW TO LIVE
FOREVER. EVERY DAY THAT WE
ARE TOGETHER, I WILL TELL
YOU A NEW SECRET. SO DON'T
WORRY KYLA!

KYLA HUGGED DADDY,
"OH THANK YOU DADDY!"

"IN FACT, KYLA, I'M ALLERGIC TO DYING."
DADDY ADDED.

"YEA, I'M ALLERGIC TO DYING TOO."
CONFIRMED KYLA.

DADDY OPENED THE REFRIGERATOR AND SPRAYED WHIPPED CREAM INTO HIS MOUTH.
WHIPPED

"HERE IS THE FIRST SECRET...EATING WHIPPED CREAM STRAIGHT FROM THE BOTTLE."

"DADDY, WILL THIS HELP ME TO LIVE FOREVER? KYLA ASKED THROUGH A MOUTHFUL OF WHIPPED CREAM."

"IT SURE WILL," DADDY REPLIED AS HE GAVE KYLA SOME WHIPPED CREAM. "PEOPLE WHO HAVE MORE FUN WILL LIVE LONGER, AND ISN'T THIS FUN!"

"YES, DADDY, CAN I PLEASE HAVE SOME MORE?" ASKED KYLA.

"OF COURSE! HERE YOU GO." ANSWERED DADDY.

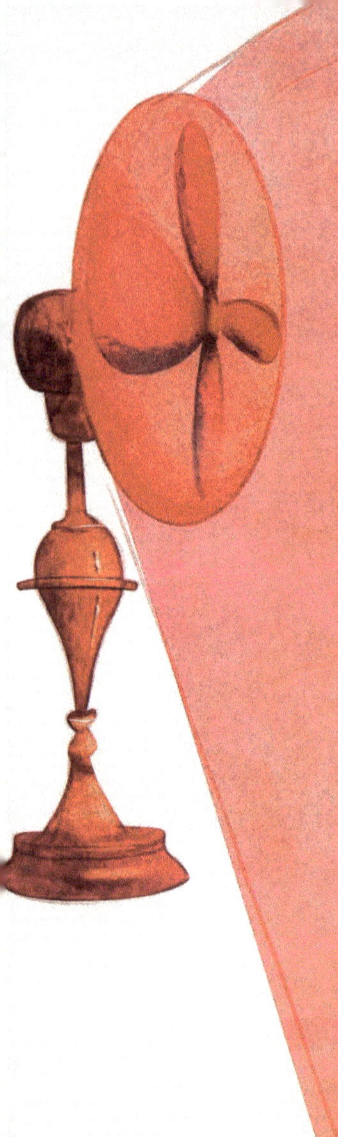

THE FOLLOWING DAY, KYLA ASKED "DADDY, CAN YOU TEACH ME ANOTHER SECRET?"

"SURE," DADDY REPLIED, "WHEN I WAS A BOY, I INVENTED A 'BUBBLE HOUSE' USING A FAN AND A BED SHEET. GO GET YOUR DOLLS AND LET'S HAVE A TEA PARTY IN THE BUBBLE HOUSE."

"YAY," KYLA EXCLAIMED, "THIS IS FUN! WE'RE INSIDE A REAL BUBBLE HOUSE! I WANT TO DO THIS FOREVER!"

FOR THE NEXT FEW YEARS, EVERY DAY THAT DADDY AND KYLA WERE TOGETHER, THEY FOUND NEW FUN AND EXCITING THINGS TO DO AND GAMES TO PLAY.

THEY MADE SILLY FACES, THEY HAD PILLOW FIGHTS, THEY PLAYED "THE FLOOR IS LAVA" TO KEEP THE BALLOONS OFF THE FLOOR, THEY PLAYED HIDE AND SEEK, THEY CREATED SCAVENGER HUNTS, THEY JUMPED ON THE TRAMPOLINE, THEY CREATED NEW MUSICAL INSTRUMENTS TO PLAY OR EVEN JUST WATCHED TV TOGETHER.

THEY LAUGHED AND LAUGHED. DADDY TAUGHT KYLA
THAT SOMETIMES IT'S OK TO EAT DESSERT FIRST,
SINCE IT'S THE BEST PART OF THE MEAL.

OCCASIONALLY KYLA WOULD ASK,
"DADDY, WILL DOING THIS HELP US TO LIVE
FOREVER?"

TO WHICH DADDY WOULD REPLY EVERY TIME,
"OH YES, ABSOLUTELY."

AS KYLA GOT OLDER, THE ACTIVITIES CHANGED TO ONES THAT OLDER KIDS DO.

DADDY WOULD HELP KYLA WITH HER HOMEWORK. DADDY AND KYLA WOULD RIDE BIKES AROUND THE NEIGHBORHOOD. DADDY TAUGHT KYLA HOW TO MAKE PANCAKES AND FLIP THEM OVER IN THE AIR FROM THE FRYING PAN.

ON THE WEEKENDS, THEY WOULD SURPRISE MOMMY WITH BREAKFAST IN BED. DADDY TAUGHT KYLA HOW TO HIT A SOFTBALL. EVERY NOW AND THEN, DADDY AND KYLA WOULD GET SOME HELIUM BALLOONS AND TALK TO EACH OTHER IN CHIPMUNK VOICES.

NO MATTER WHAT THEY DID,
THEY WOULD LAUGH AND LAUGH.

AS THE YEARS WENT BY, KYLA BECAME A GROWN UP AND HAD A FAMILY OF HER OWN, AND DADDY BECAME AN OLD MAN. HOWEVER, THAT DIDN'T STOP KYLA FROM MAKING TIME TO SPEND WITH HER DADDY, JUST LIKE SHE HAD DONE HER WHOLE LIFE.

AT THIS POINT, THEIR FAVORITE ACTIVITIES WERE NOW SIMPLY TAKING WALKS TOGETHER, OR EVEN JUST SITTING ON A PARK BENCH AND TALKING. THEY WOULD TALK ABOUT LIFE, ABOUT THE WORLD, ABOUT WHAT ALL THE GRANDKIDS ARE UP TO AND ABOUT THE FUTURE.

ONE DAY KYLA SAID, "DADDY, I LOVE YOU VERY MUCH AND I WANT TO GIVE YOU SOMETHING." KYLA REACHED INTO HER BAG. SURE ENOUGH, SHE PULLED OUT A BOTTLE OF WHIPPED CREAM. "DADDY, WHEN I WAS LITTLE, YOU TAUGHT ME THAT THIS WILL HELP PEOPLE TO LIVE FOREVER."

"KYLA SWEETIE," DADDY REPLIED, "I HAVE TO ADMIT SOMETHING TO YOU..."

KYLA INTERRUPTED...
"IT'S OK DADDY, BY NOW I ALREADY FIGURED
IT OUT. I KNOW THAT EATING WHIPPED
CREAM FROM THE BOTTLE DOESN'T
ACTUALLY MAKE SOMEONE LIVE FOREVER."

"WELL, ACTUALLY IN A WAY IT DOES", DADDY
CORRECTED KYLA.

KYLA INQUIRED, "WHAT DO YOU MEAN?"

DADDY EXPLAINED, "YOU KNOW ALL THE WONDERFUL MEMORIES WE FORMED ALL THESE YEARS? THOSE MEMORIES WILL LIVE ON FOREVER. PARENTS GET TO LIVE ON THROUGH THEIR CHILDREN'S MEMORIES. SO, NO MATTER WHERE I AM OR WHERE I'LL BE, KNOW THAT I WILL ALWAYS BE IN YOUR HEART. EVEN WHEN SOME DAY WE ARE APART, I WILL ALWAYS BE WITH YOU..."

" AFTER ALL...," DADDY SAID,
"I AM ALLERGIC TO DYING
AND SO ARE YOU."

HERE'S
HOW TO
LIVE
FOREVER

ABOUT THE AUTHOR

DAN COUSIN IS A PULITZER PRIZE-WANTER, ITALIAN-VISITED AUTHOR WHO IS ONE OF THE MOST TALKED-ABOUT ARTISTS IN THIS PARAGRAPH. ACTUALLY, DR. DANIEL COUSIN IS A MEDICAL DOCTOR TRAINED AT HARVARD, YALE, COLUMBIA AND A FEW OTHER PLACES. HE IS A MUSICIAN, A JUGGLER AND A FEW OTHER THINGS. HOWEVER, THIS IS HIS FIRST KID'S BOOK. DR. DAN WOULD LIKE TO DEDICATE THIS BOOK TO HIS AMAZING FAMILY.